INDIAN COOKBOOK 2021

HEALTHY AND TASTY INDIAN RECIPES

JANET GIUBILEO

Table of Contents

Anjeer Dry Chicken

(Dry Chicken with Figs)

Serves 4

Ingredients

750g/1lb 10oz chicken, chopped into 12 pieces

4 tbsp ghee

2 large onions, finely chopped

250ml/8fl oz water

Salt to taste

For the marinade:

10 dry figs, soaked for 1 hour

1 tsp ginger paste

1 tsp garlic paste

200g/7oz yoghurt

1½ tsp garam masala

2 tbsp single cream

Method

- Mix all the marinade ingredients together. Marinate the chicken with this mixture for an hour.

- Heat the ghee in a saucepan. Fry the onions on a medium heat till brown.

- Add the marinated chicken, water and salt. Mix well, cover with a lid and simmer for 40 minutes. Serve hot.

Chicken Yoghurt

Serves 4

Ingredients

30g/1oz mint leaves, finely chopped

30g/1oz coriander leaves, chopped

2 tsp ginger paste

2 tsp garlic paste

400g/14oz yoghurt

200g/7oz tomato purée

Juice of 1 lemon

1kg/2¼lb chicken, chopped into 12 pieces

2 tbsp refined vegetable oil

4 large onions, finely chopped

Salt to taste

Method

- Grind the mint leaves and coriander leaves to a fine paste. Mix this with the ginger paste, garlic paste, yoghurt, tomato purée and lemon juice. Marinate the chicken with this mixture for 3 hours.

- Heat the oil in a saucepan. Fry the onions on a medium heat till brown.

- Add the marinated chicken. Cover with a lid and simmer for 40 minutes, stirring occasionally. Serve hot.

Spicy Fried Chicken

Serves 4

Ingredients

1 tsp ginger paste

2 tsp garlic paste

2 green chillies, finely chopped

1 tsp chilli powder

1 tsp garam masala

2 tsp lemon juice

½ tsp turmeric

Salt to taste

1kg/2¼lb chicken, chopped into 8 pieces

Refined vegetable oil for deep-frying

Breadcrumbs, to coat

Method

- Mix the ginger paste, garlic paste, green chillies, chilli powder, garam masala, lemon juice, turmeric and salt together. Marinate the chicken with this mixture for 3 hours.

- Heat the oil in a frying pan. Coat each marinated chicken piece with the breadcrumbs and deep fry on a medium heat till golden brown.

- Drain on absorbent paper and serve hot.

Chicken Supreme

Serves 4

Ingredients

1 tsp ginger paste

1 tsp garlic paste

1kg/2¼lb chicken, chopped into 8 pieces

200g/7oz yoghurt

Salt to taste

250ml/8fl oz water

2 tbsp refined vegetable oil

2 large onions, sliced

4 red chillies

5cm/2in cinnamon

2 black cardamom pods

4 cloves

1 tbsp chana dhal*, dry roasted

Method

- Mix the ginger paste and garlic paste together. Marinate the chicken with this mixture for 30 minutes. Add the yoghurt, salt and water. Set aside.

- Heat the oil in a saucepan. Add the onions, chillies, cinnamon, cardamom, cloves and chana dhal. Fry for 3-4 minutes on a low heat.

- Grind to a paste and add to the chicken mixture. Mix well.

- Cook on a low heat for 30 minutes. Serve hot.

Chicken Vindaloo

(Spicy Goan-style Chicken Curry)

Serves 4

Ingredients

60ml/2fl oz malt vinegar

1 tbsp cumin seeds

1 tsp peppercorns

6 red chillies

1 tsp turmeric

Salt to taste

4 tbsp refined vegetable oil

3 large onions, finely chopped

1kg/2¼lb chicken, chopped into 8 pieces

Method

- Grind the vinegar with the cumin seeds, peppercorns, chillies, turmeric and salt to a smooth paste. Set aside.

- Heat the oil in a saucepan. Add the onions and fry till translucent. Add the vinegar-cumin seeds paste. Mix well and fry for 4-5 minutes.

- Add the chicken and cook on a low heat for 30 minutes. Serve hot.

Caramelized Chicken

Serves 4

Ingredients

200g/7oz yoghurt

1 tsp ginger paste

1 tsp garlic paste

2 tbsp ground coriander

1 tsp ground cumin

1½ tsp garam masala

Salt to taste

1kg/2¼lb chicken, chopped into 8 pieces

3 tbsp refined vegetable oil

2 tsp sugar

3 cloves

2.5cm/1in cinnamon

6 black peppercorns

Method

- Mix together the yoghurt, ginger paste, garlic paste, ground coriander, ground cumin, garam masala and salt. Marinate the chicken with this mixture overnight.

- Heat the oil in a saucepan. Add the sugar, cloves, cinnamon and peppercorns. Fry for a minute. Add the marinated chicken and cook on a low heat for 40 minutes. Serve hot.

Cashew Chicken

Serves 4

Ingredients

1kg/2¼lb chicken, chopped into 12 pieces

Salt to taste

1 tsp ginger paste

1 tsp garlic paste

4 tbsp refined vegetable oil

4 large onions, sliced

15 cashew nuts, ground to a paste

6 red chillies, soaked for 15 minutes

2 tsp ground cumin

60ml/2fl oz ketchup

500ml/16fl oz water

Method

- Marinate the chicken with the salt and ginger and garlic pastes for 1 hour.

- Heat the oil in a saucepan. Fry the onions on a medium heat till brown.

- Add the cashew nuts, chillies, cumin and ketchup. Cook for 5 minutes.

- Add the chicken and the water. Simmer for 40 minutes and serve hot.

Quick Chicken

Serves 4

Ingredients

4 tbsp refined vegetable oil

6 red chillies

6 black peppercorns

1 tsp coriander seeds

1 tsp cumin seeds

2.5cm/1in cinnamon

4 cloves

1 tsp turmeric

8 garlic cloves

1 tsp tamarind paste

4 medium-sized onions, finely sliced

2 large tomatoes, finely chopped

1kg/2¼lb chicken, chopped into 12 pieces

250ml/8fl oz water

Salt to taste

Method

- Heat half a tbsp of oil in a saucepan. Add the red chillies, peppercorns, coriander seeds, cumin seeds, cinnamon and cloves. Fry them on a medium heat for 2-3 minutes.

- Add the turmeric, garlic and tamarind paste. Grind the mixture to a smooth paste. Set aside.

- Heat the remaining oil in a saucepan. Add the onions and fry them on a medium heat till they are brown. Add the tomatoes and sauté for 3-4 minutes.

- Add the chicken and sauté for 4-5 minutes.

- Add the water and salt. Mix well and cover with a lid. Simmer for 40 minutes, stirring occasionally.

- Serve hot.

Coorgi Chicken Curry

Serves 4

Ingredients

1kg/2¼lb chicken, chopped into 12 pieces

Salt to taste

1 tsp turmeric

50g/1¾oz grated coconut

3 tbsp refined vegetable oil

1 tsp garlic paste

2 large onions, finely sliced

1 tsp ground cumin

1 tsp ground coriander

360ml/12fl oz water

Method

- Marinate the chicken with the salt and turmeric for an hour. Set aside.
- Grind the coconut with enough water to form a smooth paste.
- Heat the oil in a saucepan. Add the coconut paste with the garlic paste, onions, ground cumin and coriander. Fry on a low heat for 4-5 minutes.
- Add the marinated chicken. Mix well and fry for 4-5 minutes. Add the water, cover with a lid and simmer for 40 minutes. Serve hot.

Pan Chicken

Serves 4

Ingredients

4 tbsp refined vegetable oil

1 tsp ginger paste

1 tsp garlic paste

2 large onions, finely chopped

1 tsp garam masala

1½ tbsp cashew nuts, ground

1½ tbsp melon seeds*, ground

1 tsp ground coriander

500g/1lb 2oz boneless chicken

200g/7oz tomato purée

2 chicken stock cubes

250ml/8fl oz water

Salt to taste

Method

- Heat the oil in a saucepan. Add the ginger paste, garlic paste, onions and garam masala. Fry for 2-3 minutes on a low heat. Add the cashew nuts, melon seeds and ground coriander. Fry for 2 minutes.
- Add the chicken and fry for 5 minutes. Add the tomato purée, stock cubes, water and salt. Cover and simmer for 40 minutes. Serve hot.

Spinach Chicken

Serves 4

Ingredients

3 tbsp refined vegetable oil

6 cloves

5cm/2in cinnamon

2 bay leaves

2 large onions, finely chopped

12 garlic cloves, finely chopped

400g/14oz spinach, coarsely chopped

200g/7oz yoghurt

250ml/8fl oz water

750g/1lb 10oz chicken, chopped into 8 pieces

Salt to taste

Method

- Heat 2 tbsp oil in a saucepan. Add the cloves, cinnamon and bay leaves. Let them splutter for 15 seconds.
- Add the onions and fry them on a medium heat till they turn translucent.
- Add the garlic and spinach. Mix well. Cook for 5-6 minutes. Cool and grind with enough water to make a smooth paste.
- Heat the remaining oil in a saucepan. Add the spinach paste and fry for 3-4 minutes. Add the yoghurt and water. Cook for 5-6 minutes. Add the chicken and salt. Cook on a low heat for 40 minutes. Serve hot.

Chicken Indienne

Serves 4

Ingredients

4-5 tbsp refined vegetable oil

4 large onions, minced

1kg/2¼lb chicken, chopped into 10 pieces

Salt to taste

500ml/16fl oz water

For the spice mixture:

2.5cm/1in root ginger

10 garlic cloves

1 tbsp garam masala

2 tsp fennel seeds

1½ tbsp coriander seeds

60ml/2fl oz water

Method

- Grind the spice mixture ingredients into a smooth paste. Set aside.

- Heat the oil in a saucepan. Fry the onions on a medium heat till brown.

- Add the spice mixture paste, the chicken and salt. Fry for 5-6 minutes. Add the water. Cover and cook for 40 minutes. Serve hot.

Kori Gassi

(Mangalorean Chicken with Curry)

Serves 4

Ingredients

4 tbsp refined vegetable oil

6 whole red chillies

1 tsp black peppercorns

4 tsp coriander seeds

2 tsp cumin seeds

150g/5½oz fresh coconut, grated

8 garlic cloves

500ml/16fl oz water

3 large onions, finely chopped

1 tsp turmeric

1kg/2¼lb chicken, chopped into 8 pieces

2 tsp tamarind paste

Salt to taste

Method

- Heat 1 tsp oil in a saucepan. Add the red chillies, peppercorns, coriander seeds and cumin seeds. Let them splutter for 15 seconds.

- Grind this mixture to a paste with the coconut, garlic and half the water.

- Heat the remaining oil in a saucepan. Add the onions, turmeric and the coconut paste. Fry on a medium heat for 5-6 minutes.

- Add the chicken, tamarind paste, salt and the remaining water. Mix well. Cover with a lid and simmer for 40 minutes. Serve hot.

Chicken Ghezado

(Goan-style Chicken)

Serves 4

Ingredients

3 tbsp refined vegetable oil

2 large onions, finely chopped

1 tsp ginger paste

1 tsp garlic paste

2 tomatoes, finely chopped

1kg/2¼lb chicken, chopped into 8 pieces

1 tbsp ground coriander

2 tbsp garam masala

Salt to taste

250ml/8fl oz water

Method

- Heat the oil in a saucepan. Add the onions, ginger paste and garlic paste. Fry for 2 minutes. Add the tomatoes and chicken. Fry for 5 minutes.
- Add all the remaining ingredients. Simmer for 40 minutes and serve hot.

Chicken in Tomato Gravy

Serves 4

Ingredients

1 tbsp ghee

2.5cm/1in root ginger, finely chopped

10 garlic cloves, finely chopped

2 large onions, finely chopped

4 red chillies

1 tsp garam masala

1 tsp turmeric

800g/1¾lb tomato purée

1kg/2¼lb chicken, chopped into 8 pieces

Salt to taste

200g/7oz yoghurt

Method

- Heat the ghee in a saucepan. Add the ginger, garlic, onions, red chillies, garam masala and turmeric. Fry on a medium heat for 3 minutes.
- Add the tomato purée and fry for 4 minutes on a low heat.
- Add the chicken, salt and yoghurt. Mix thoroughly.
- Cover and simmer for 40 minutes, stirring occasionally. Serve hot.

Shahenshah Murgh

(Chicken cooked in Special Gravy)

Serves 4

Ingredients

250g/9oz peanuts, soaked for 4 hours

60g/2oz raisins

4 green chillies, slit lengthways

1 tbsp cumin seeds

4 tbsp ghee

1 tbsp ground cinnamon

3 large onions, finely chopped

1kg/2¼lb chicken, chopped in 12 pieces

Salt to taste

Method

- Drain the peanuts and grind them with the raisins, green chillies, cumin seeds and enough water to form a smooth paste. Set aside.
- Heat the ghee in a saucepan. Add the ground cinnamon. Let it splutter for 30 seconds.
- Add the onions and the ground peanut-raisin paste. Fry for 2-3 minutes.
- Add the chicken and salt. Mix well. Cook on a low heat for 40 minutes, stirring occasionally. Serve hot.

Chicken do Pyaaza

(Chicken with Onions)

Serves 4

Ingredients

4 tbsp ghee plus extra for deep frying

4 cloves

½ tsp fennel seeds

1 tsp ground coriander

1 tsp ground black pepper

2.5cm/1in root ginger, finely chopped

8 garlic cloves, finely chopped

4 large onions, sliced

1kg/2¼lb chicken, chopped into 12 pieces

½ tsp turmeric

4 tomatoes, finely chopped

Salt to taste

Method

- Heat 4 tbsp ghee in a saucepan. Add the cloves, fennel seeds, ground coriander and pepper. Let them splutter for 15 seconds.
- Add the ginger, garlic and onions. Fry on a medium heat for 1-2 minutes.
- Add the chicken, turmeric, tomatoes and salt. Mix well. Cook on a low heat for 30 minutes, stirring frequently. Serve hot.

Bengali Chicken

Serves 4

Ingredients

300g/10oz yoghurt

1 tsp ginger paste

1 tsp garlic paste

3 large onions, 1 grated plus 2 finely chopped

1 tsp turmeric

2 tsp chilli powder

Salt to taste

1kg/2¼lb chicken, chopped into 12 pieces

4 tbsp mustard oil

500ml/16fl oz water

Method

- Mix the yoghurt, ginger paste, garlic paste, onion, turmeric, chilli powder and salt together. Marinate the chicken with this mixture for 30 minutes.

- Heat the oil in a saucepan. Add the chopped onions and fry till brown.

- Add the marinated chicken, water and salt. Mix well. Cover with a lid and simmer for 40 minutes. Serve hot.

Lasooni Murgh

(Chicken cooked with Garlic)

Serves 4

Ingredients

200g/7oz yoghurt

2 tbsp garlic paste

1 tsp garam masala

2 tbsp lemon juice

1 tsp ground black pepper

5 saffron strands

Salt to taste

750g/1lb 10oz boneless chicken, chopped into 8 pieces

2 tbsp refined vegetable oil

60ml/2fl oz double cream

Method

- Mix together the yoghurt, garlic paste, garam masala, lemon juice, pepper, saffron, salt and chicken. Refrigerate the mixture overnight.

- Heat the oil in a saucepan. Add the chicken mixture, cover with a lid and cook on a low heat for 40 minutes, stirring occasionally.

- Add the cream and stir for a minute. Serve hot.

Chicken Cafreal

(Goan Chicken in a Coriander Sauce)

Serves 4

Ingredients

1kg/2¼lb chicken, chopped into 8 pieces

5 tbsp refined vegetable oil

250ml/8fl oz water

Salt to taste

4 lemons, quartered

For the marinade:

50g/1¾oz coriander leaves, chopped

2.5cm/1in root ginger

10 garlic cloves

120ml/4fl oz malt vinegar

1 tbsp garam masala

Method

- Mix all the marinade ingredients together and grind with enough water to form a smooth paste. Marinate the chicken with this mixture for an hour.

- Heat the oil in a saucepan. Add the marinated chicken and fry on a medium heat for 5 minutes. Add the water and salt. Cover with a lid and simmer for 40 minutes, stirring occasionally. Serve hot with the lemons.

Chicken with Apricots

Serves 4

Ingredients

4 tbsp refined vegetable oil

3 large onions, finely sliced

1 tsp ginger paste

1 tsp garlic paste

1kg/2¼lb chicken, chopped into 8 pieces

1 tsp chilli powder

1 tsp turmeric

2 tsp ground cumin

2 tbsp sugar

300g/10oz dried apricots, soaked for 10 minutes

60ml/2fl oz water

1 tbsp malt vinegar

Salt to taste

Method

- Heat the oil in a saucepan. Add the onions, ginger paste and garlic paste. Fry on a medium heat till the onions are brown.
- Add the chicken, chilli powder, turmeric, ground cumin and sugar. Mix well and fry for 5-6 minutes.
- Add the remaining ingredients. Simmer for 40 minutes and serve hot.

Grilled Chicken

Serves 4

Ingredients

Salt to taste

1 tbsp malt vinegar

1 tsp ground black pepper

1 tsp ginger paste

1 tsp garlic paste

2 tsp garam masala

1kg/2¼lb chicken, chopped into 8 pieces

2 tbsp ghee

2 large onions, sliced

2 tomatoes, finely chopped

Method

- Mix the salt, vinegar, pepper, ginger paste, garlic paste and garam masala together. Marinate the chicken with this mixture for an hour.

- Heat the ghee in a saucepan. Add the onions and fry on a medium heat till they turn brown.

- Add the tomatoes and marinated chicken. Mix thoroughly and fry for 4-5 minutes.

- Remove from the heat and grill the mixture for 40 minutes. Serve hot.

Pepper Duck Roast

Serves 4

Ingredients

2 tbsp malt vinegar

1½ tsp ginger paste

1 tsp garlic paste

Salt to taste

1 tsp ground black pepper

1kg/2¼lb duck

2 tbsp butter

2 tbsp refined vegetable oil

3 large onions, finely sliced

4 tomatoes, finely chopped

1 tsp sugar

500ml/16fl oz water

Method

- Mix the vinegar, ginger paste, garlic paste, salt and pepper. Pierce the duck with a fork and marinate with this mixture for 1 hour.

- Heat the butter and oil together in a saucepan. Add the onions and tomatoes. Fry on a medium heat for 3-4 minutes. Add the duck, sugar and water. Mix well and simmer for 45 minutes. Serve hot.

Bhuna Chicken

(Chicken cooked in Yoghurt)

Serves 4

Ingredients

4 tbsp refined vegetable oil

1kg/2¼lb chicken, chopped into 12 pieces

1 tsp ginger paste

1 tsp garlic paste

½ tsp turmeric

2 large onions, finely chopped

1½ tsp garam masala

1 tsp freshly ground black pepper

150g/5½oz yoghurt, whisked

Salt to taste

Method

- Heat the oil in a saucepan. Add the chicken and fry on a medium heat for 6-7 minutes. Drain and set aside.
- To the same oil, add the ginger paste, garlic paste, turmeric and onions. Fry on a medium heat for 2 minutes, stirring frequently.
- Add the fried chicken and all the remaining ingredients. Cook for 40 minutes on a low heat. Serve hot.

Chicken Curry with Eggs

Serves 4

Ingredients

6 garlic cloves

2.5cm/1in root ginger

25g/scant 1oz grated fresh coconut

2 tsp poppy seeds

1 tsp garam masala

1 tsp cumin seeds

1 tbsp coriander seeds

1 tsp turmeric

Salt to taste

4 tbsp refined vegetable oil

2 large onions, finely chopped

1kg/2¼lb chicken, chopped into 8 pieces

4 eggs, hard-boiled and halved

Method

- Grind together the garlic, ginger, coconut, poppy seeds, garam masala, cumin seeds, coriander seeds, turmeric and salt. Set aside.

- Heat the oil in a saucepan. Add the onions and the ground paste. Fry on a medium heat for 3-4 minutes. Add the chicken and mix well to coat.

- Simmer for 40 minutes. Garnish with the eggs and serve hot.

Chicken Fried with Spices

Serves 4

Ingredients

1kg/2¼lb chicken, chopped into 8 pieces

250ml/8fl oz refined vegetable oil

For the marinade:

1½ tsp ground coriander

4 green cardamom pods

7.5cm/3in cinnamon

½ tsp fennel seeds

1 tbsp garam masala

4-6 garlic cloves

2.5cm/1in root ginger

1 large onion, grated

1 large tomato, puréed

Salt to taste

Method

- Grind all the marinade ingredients together. Marinate the chicken with this mixture for 30 minutes.
- Cook the marinated chicken in a saucepan on a medium heat for 30 minutes, stirring occasionally.
- Heat the oil and fry the cooked chicken for 5-6 minutes. Serve hot.

Goan Kombdi

(Goan Chicken Curry)

Serves 4

Ingredients

1kg/2¼lb chicken, chopped into 8 pieces

Salt to taste

½ tsp turmeric

6 red chillies

5 cloves

5cm/2in cinnamon

1 tbsp coriander seeds

½ tsp fenugreek seeds

½ tsp mustard seeds

4 tbsp oil

1 tbsp tamarind paste

500ml/16fl oz coconut milk

Method

- Marinate the chicken with the salt and turmeric for 1 hour. Set aside.
- Grind together the chillies, cloves, cinnamon, coriander seeds, fenugreek seeds and mustard seeds with enough water to form a paste.
- Heat the oil in a saucepan. Fry the paste for 4 minutes. Add the chicken, tamarind paste and coconut milk. Simmer for 40 minutes and serve hot.

South Chicken Curry

Serves 4

Ingredients

16 cashew nuts

6 red chillies

2 tbsp coriander seeds

½ tsp cumin seeds

1 tbsp lemon juice

5 tbsp ghee

3 large onions, finely chopped

10 garlic cloves, finely chopped

2.5cm/1in root ginger, finely chopped

1kg/2¼lb chicken, chopped into 12 pieces

1 tsp turmeric

Salt to taste

500ml/16fl oz coconut milk

Method

- Grind the cashew nuts, red chillies, coriander seeds, cumin seeds and lemon juice with enough water to form a smooth paste. Set aside.

- Heat the ghee. Add the onions, garlic and ginger. Fry for 2 minutes.

- Add the chicken, turmeric, salt and the cashew nut paste. Fry for 5 minutes. Add the coconut milk and simmer for 40 minutes. Serve hot.

Undhiyu

(Gujarati Mixed Vegetable with Dumplings)

Serves 4

Ingredients

2 large potatoes, peeled

250g/9oz broad beans in their pods

1 unripe banana, peeled

20g/¾oz yam, peeled

2 small aubergines

60g/2oz fresh coconut, grated

8 garlic cloves

2 green chillies

2.5cm/1in root ginger

100g/3½oz coriander leaves, finely chopped

Salt to taste

60ml/2fl oz refined vegetable oil plus extra for deep frying

Pinch of asafoetida

½ tsp mustard seeds

250ml/8fl oz water

For the muthias:

60g/2oz besan*

25g/scant 1oz fresh fenugreek leaves, finely chopped

½ tsp ginger paste

2 green chillies, finely chopped

Method

- Dice the potatoes, beans, banana, yam and aubergines. Set aside.
- Grind together the coconut, garlic, green chillies, ginger and coriander leaves to a paste. Mix this paste with the diced vegetables and salt. Set aside.
- Mix all the muthia ingredients together. Knead the mixture to a firm dough. Divide the dough into walnut-sized balls.
- Heat the oil for deep frying in a frying pan. Add the muthias. Deep fry them on a medium heat till golden brown. Drain and set aside.
- Heat the remaining oil in a saucepan. Add the asafoetida and mustard seeds. Let them splutter for 15 seconds.
- Add the water, muthias and the vegetable mixture. Mix well. Cover with a lid and simmer for 20 minutes, stirring at regular intervals. Serve hot.

Banana Kofta Curry

Serves 4

Ingredients
For the koftas:

2 unripe bananas, boiled and peeled

2 large potatoes, boiled and peeled

3 green chillies, finely chopped

1 large onion, finely chopped

1 tbsp coriander leaves, finely chopped

1 tbsp besan*

½ tsp chilli powder

Salt to taste

Ghee for deep frying

For the curry:

75g/2½oz ghee

1 large onion, finely chopped

10 garlic cloves, crushed

1 tbsp ground coriander

1 tsp garam masala

2 tomatoes, finely chopped

3 curry leaves

Salt to taste

250ml/8fl oz water

½ tbsp coriander leaves, finely chopped

Method

- Mash the bananas and potatoes together.
- Mix with the remaining kofta ingredients, except the ghee. Knead this mixture to a firm dough. Divide the dough into walnut-sized balls to make the koftas.
- Heat the ghee for deep frying in a frying pan. Add the koftas. Fry them on a medium heat till they turn golden brown. Drain and set aside.
- For the curry, heat the ghee in a saucepan. Add the onion and garlic. Fry on a medium heat till the onion turns translucent. Add the ground coriander and garam masala. Fry for 2-3 minutes.
- Add the tomatoes, curry leaves, salt and water. Mix well. Simmer the mixture for 15 minutes, stirring occasionally.
- Add the fried koftas. Cover with a lid and continue to simmer for 2-3 minutes.
- Garnish with the coriander leaves. Serve hot.

Bitter Gourd with Onion

Serves 4

Ingredients

500g/1lb 2oz bitter gourds*

Salt to taste

750ml/1¼ pints water

4 tbsp refined vegetable oil

½ tsp cumin seeds

½ tsp mustard seeds

Pinch of asafoetida

½ tsp ginger paste

½ tsp garlic paste

2 large onions, finely chopped

½ tsp turmeric

1 tsp chilli powder

1 tsp ground cumin

1 tsp ground coriander

1 tsp sugar

Juice of 1 lemon

1 tbsp coriander leaves, finely chopped

Method

- Peel the bitter gourds and slice them into thin rings. Discard the seeds.
- Cook them with the salt and water in a saucepan on a medium heat for 5-7 minutes. Remove from the heat, drain and squeeze out the water, set aside.
- Heat the oil in a saucepan. Add the cumin and mustard seeds. Let them splutter for 15 seconds.
- Add the asafoetida, ginger paste and garlic paste. Fry the mixture on a medium heat for a minute.
- Add the onions. Fry them for 2-3 minutes.
- Add the turmeric, chilli powder, ground cumin and ground coriander. Mix well.

- Add the bitter gourd, sugar and lemon juice. Mix thoroughly. Cover with a lid and cook the mixture on a low heat for 6-7 minutes, stirring at regular intervals.
- Garnish with the coriander leaves. Serve hot.

Sukha Khatta Chana

(Dry Sour Chickpeas)

Serves 4

Ingredients

4 black peppercorns

2 cloves

2.5cm/1in cinnamon

½ tsp coriander seeds

½ tsp black cumin seeds

½ tsp cumin seeds

500g/1lb 2oz chickpeas, soaked overnight

Salt to taste

1 litre/1¾ pints water

1 tbsp dried pomegranate seeds

Salt to taste

1cm/½in root ginger, finely chopped

1 green chilli, chopped

2 tsp tamarind paste

2 tbsp ghee

1 small potato, diced

1 tomato, finely chopped

Method

- For the spice mixture, grind together the peppercorns, cloves, cinnamon, coriander, black cumin seeds and cumin seeds to a fine powder. Set aside.
- Mix the chickpeas with the salt and water. Cook this mixture in a saucepan on a medium heat for 45 minutes. Set aside.
- Dry roast the pomegranate seeds in a frying pan on a medium heat for 2-3 minutes. Remove from the heat and grind to a powder. Mix with the salt and dry roast the mixture again for 5 minutes. Transfer to a saucepan.
- Add the ginger, green chilli and tamarind paste. Cook this mixture on a medium heat for 4-5 minutes. Add the ground spice mixture. Mix thoroughly and set aside.
- Heat the ghee in another pan. Add the potatoes. Fry them on a medium heat till golden brown.
- Add the fried potatoes to the cooked chickpeas. Also add the tamarind-ground spice mixture.
- Mix thoroughly and cook on a low heat for 5-6 minutes.

Bharwan Karela

(Stuffed Bitter Gourd)

Serves 4

Ingredients

500g/1lb 2oz small bitter gourds*

Salt to taste

1 tsp turmeric

Refined vegetable oil for deep frying

For the stuffing:

5-6 green chillies

2.5cm/1in root ginger

12 garlic cloves

3 small onions

1 tbsp refined vegetable oil

4 large potatoes, boiled and mashed

½ tsp turmeric

½ tsp chilli powder

1 tsp ground cumin

1 tsp ground coriander

Pinch of asafoetida

Salt to taste

Method

- Peel the bitter gourds. Slit them lengthways carefully, keeping the bases intact. Remove the seeds and the pulp and discard them. Rub the salt and turmeric on the outer shells. Set them aside for 4-5 hours.
- For the stuffing, grind together the chillies, ginger, garlic and onions to a paste. Set aside.
- Heat 1 tbsp oil in a frying pan. Add the onion-ginger-garlic paste. Fry it on a medium heat for 2-3 minutes.
- Add the remaining stuffing ingredients. Mix well. Fry the mixture on a medium heat for 3-4 minutes.
- Remove from the heat and cool the mixture. Stuff this mixture into the gourds. Tie each gourd with a thread so the stuffing does not fall out while cooking.
- Heat the oil for deep frying in a pan. Add the stuffed gourds. Fry them on a medium heat till they turn brown and crispy, turning them frequently.
- Untie the bitter gourds and discard the threads. Serve hot.

Cabbage Kofta Curry

(Cabbage Dumplings in Sauce)

Serves 4

Ingredients

1 large cabbage, grated

250g/9oz besan*

Salt to taste

Refined vegetable oil for deep frying

2 tbsp coriander leaves, to garnish

For the sauce:

3 tbsp refined vegetable oil

3 bay leaves

1 black cardamom

1cm/½in cinnamon

1 clove

1 large onion,

finely chopped

2.5cm/1in root ginger, julienned

3 tomatoes, finely chopped

74

1 tsp ground coriander

1 tsp ground cumin

Salt to taste

250ml/8fl oz water

Method

- Knead together the cabbage, besan and salt to a soft dough. Divide the dough into walnut-sized balls.
- Heat the oil in a frying pan. Add the balls. Deep fry them on a medium heat till they turn golden brown. Drain and set aside.
- For the sauce, heat the oil in a saucepan. Add the bay leaves, cardamom, cinnamon and clove. Let them splutter for 30 seconds.
- Add the onion and ginger. Fry this mixture on a medium heat till the onion turns translucent.
- Add the tomatoes, ground coriander and ground cumin. Mix well. Fry for 2-3 minutes.
- Add the salt and water. Stir for a minute. Cover with a lid and simmer for 5 minutes.
- Uncover the pan and add the kofta balls. Simmer for 5 more minutes, stirring occasionally.
- Garnish with the coriander leaves. Serve hot.

Pineapple Gojju

(Spicy Pineapple Compote)

Serves 4

Ingredients

3 tbsp refined vegetable oil

250ml/8fl oz water

1 tsp mustard seeds

6 curry leaves, crushed

Pinch of asafoetida

½ tsp turmeric

Salt to taste

400g/14oz pineapple, chopped

For the spice mixture:

4 tbsp fresh coconut, grated

3 green chillies

2 red chillies

½ tsp fennel seeds

½ tsp fenugreek seeds

1 tsp cumin seeds

2 tsp coriander seeds

1 small bunch coriander leaves

1 clove

2-3 peppercorns

Method

- Mix all the spice mixture ingredients together.
- Heat 1 tbsp of the oil in a saucepan. Add the spice mixture. Fry it on a medium heat for 1-2 minutes, stirring frequently. Remove from the heat and grind with half the water to a smooth paste. Set aside.
- Heat the remaining oil in a saucepan. Add the mustard seeds and curry leaves. Let them splutter for 15 seconds.
- Add the asafoetida, turmeric and salt. Fry for a minute.
- Add the pineapple, the spice mixture paste and the remaining water. Mix well. Cover with a lid and simmer for 8-12 minutes. Serve hot.

Bitter Gourd Gojju

(Spicy Bitter Gourd Compote)

Serves 4

Ingredients

Salt to taste

4 large bitter gourds*, peeled, slit lengthways, deseeded and sliced

6 tbsp refined vegetable oil

1 tsp mustard seeds

8-10 curry leaves

1 large onion, grated

3-4 garlic cloves, crushed

2 tsp chilli powder

1 tsp ground cumin

½ tsp turmeric

1 tsp ground coriander

2 tsp sambhar powder*

2 tsp fresh coconut, shredded

1 tsp fenugreek seeds, dry roasted and ground

2 tsp white sesame seeds, dry roasted and ground

2 tbsp jaggery*, melted

½ tsp tamarind paste

250ml/8fl oz water

Pinch of asafoetida

Method

- Rub the salt on the bitter gourd slices. Place them in a bowl and seal it with foil. Set aside for 30 minutes. Squeeze out any excess moisture.

- Heat half the oil in a saucepan. Add the bitter gourds. Fry them on a medium heat till they turn golden brown. Set aside.

- Heat the remaining oil in another saucepan. Add the mustard seeds and curry leaves. Let them splutter for 15 seconds.

- Add the onion and garlic. Fry this mixture on a medium heat till the onion turns brown.

- Add the chilli powder, ground cumin, turmeric, ground coriander, sambhar powder and coconut. Fry for 2-3 minutes.

- Add the remaining ingredients, except the water and asafoetida. Fry for another minute.

- Add the fried bitter gourds, some salt and the water. Mix well. Cover with a lid and simmer for 12-15 minutes.

- Add the asafoetida. Mix well. Serve hot.

Baingan Mirchi ka Salan

(Aubergine and Chilli)

Serves 4

Ingredients

6 whole green peppers

4 tbsp refined vegetable oil

600g/1lb 5oz small aubergines, quartered

4 green chillies

1 tsp sesame seeds

10 cashew nuts

20-25 peanuts

5 black peppercorns

¼ tsp fenugreek seeds

¼ tsp mustard seeds

1 tsp ginger paste

1 tsp garlic paste

1 tsp ground coriander

1 tsp ground cumin

½ tsp turmeric

125g/4½oz yoghurt

2 tsp tamarind paste

3 whole red chillies

Salt to taste

1 litre/1¾ pints water

Method

- Deseed and chop the green peppers into long strips.
- Heat 1 tbsp oil in a saucepan. Add the green peppers and sauté them on a medium heat for 1-2 minutes. Set aside.
- Heat 2 tbsp oil in another saucepan. Add the aubergines and green chillies. Sauté on a medium heat for 2-3 minutes. Set aside.
- Heat a frying pan and dry roast the sesame seeds, cashew nuts, peanuts and peppercorns on a medium heat for 1-2 minutes. Remove from the heat and grind the mixture coarsely.
- Heat the remaining oil in a saucepan. Add the fenugreek seeds, mustard seeds, ginger paste, garlic paste, ground coriander, ground cumin, turmeric and the sesame seeds-cashew nuts mixture. Fry on a medium heat for 2-3 minutes.
- Add the sautéed green peppers, the sautéed aubergines and all the remaining ingredients. Simmer for 10-12 minutes.
- Serve hot.

Chicken with Greens

Serves 4

Ingredients

750g/1lb 10oz chicken, chopped into 8 pieces

50g/1¾oz spinach, finely chopped

25g/scant 1oz fresh fenugreek leaves, finely chopped

100g/3½oz coriander leaves, finely chopped

50g/1¾oz mint leaves, finely chopped

6 green chillies, finely chopped

120ml/4fl oz refined vegetable oil

2-3 large onions, finely sliced

Salt to taste

Method

- Mix all the marinade ingredients together. Marinate the chicken with this mixture for an hour.
- Grind together the spinach, fenugreek leaves, coriander leaves and mint leaves with the green chillies to a smooth paste. Mix this paste with the marinated chicken. Set aside.
- Heat the oil in a saucepan. Add the onions. Fry them on a medium heat till they turn brown.

- Add the chicken mixture and the salt. Mix well. Cover with a lid and cook on a low heat for 40 minutes, stirring occasionally. Serve hot.

For the marinade:

1 tsp garam masala

1 tsp ground coriander

1 tsp ground cumin

200g/7oz yoghurt

¼ tsp turmeric

1 tsp chilli powder

1 tsp ginger paste

1 tsp garlic paste

Chicken Tikka Masala

Serves 4

Ingredients

200g/7oz yoghurt

½ tbsp ginger paste

½ tbsp garlic paste

Dash of orange food colour

2 tbsp refined vegetable oil

500g/1lb 2oz boneless chicken, chopped into bite-sized pieces

1 tbsp butter

6 tomatoes, finely chopped

2 large onions

½ tsp ginger paste

½ tsp garlic paste

½ tsp turmeric

1 tbsp garam masala

1 tsp chilli powder

Salt to taste

1 tbsp coriander leaves, finely chopped

Method

- For the tikka, mix together the yoghurt, ginger paste, garlic paste, food colour and 1 tbsp oil. Marinate the chicken with this mixture for 5 hours.
- Grill the marinated chicken for 10 minutes. Set aside.
- Heat the butter in a saucepan. Add the tomatoes. Fry them on a medium heat for 3-4 minutes. Remove from the heat and blend to a smooth paste. Set aside.
- Grind the onion into a smooth paste.
- Heat the remaining oil in a saucepan. Add the onion paste. Fry it on a medium heat till it turns brown.

- Add the ginger paste and garlic paste. Fry for a minute.
- Add the turmeric, garam masala, chilli powder and the tomato paste. Mix well. Stirfry the mixture for 3-4 minutes.
- Add the salt and the grilled chicken. Mix gently till the sauce coats the chicken.
- Garnish with the coriander leaves. Serve hot.

Spicy Stuffed Chicken in Rich Sauce

Serves 4

Ingredients

½ tsp chilli powder

½ tsp garam masala

4 tsp ginger paste

4 tsp garlic paste

Salt to taste

8 chicken breasts, flattened

4 large onions, finely chopped

5cm/1in root ginger, finely chopped

5 green chillies, finely chopped

200g/7oz khoya*

2 tbsp lemon juice

50g/1¾oz coriander leaves, finely chopped

15 cashew nuts

5 tsp desiccated coconut

30g/1oz flaked almonds

1 tsp saffron, soaked in 1 tbsp milk

150g/5½oz ghee

200g/7oz yoghurt, whisked

Method

- Mix the chilli powder, garam masala, half the ginger paste, half the garlic paste and some salt. Marinate the chicken breasts with this mixture for 2 hours.
- Mix together half the onions with the chopped ginger, green chillies, khoya, lemon juice, salt and half the coriander leaves. Divide this mixture into 8 equal portions.
- Place each portion at the narrower end of each chicken breast and roll inwards to seal the breast. Set aside.
- Preheat the oven to 200°C (400°F, Gas Mark 6). Place the stuffed chicken breasts in a greased tray and roast them for 15-20 minutes till they turn golden brown. Set aside.
- Grind together the cashew nuts and coconut to a smooth paste. Set aside.
- Soak the almonds in the saffron milk mixture. Set aside.
- Heat the ghee in a saucepan. Add the remaining onions. Fry them on a medium heat till they turn translucent. Add the remaining ginger paste and garlic paste. Fry the mixture for a minute.
- Add the cashew nuts-coconut paste. Fry for a minute. Add the yoghurt and the roasted chicken breasts. Mix well. Cook on a low heat for 5-6 minutes, stirring frequently. Add the almond-saffron mixture. Mix gently. Simmer for 5 minutes.

- Garnish with the coriander leaves. Serve hot.

Spicy Chicken Masala

Serves 4

Ingredients

6 whole dry red chillies

2 tbsp coriander seeds

6 green cardamom pods

6 cloves

5cm/2in cinnamon

2 tsp fennel seeds

½ tsp black peppercorns

120ml/4fl oz refined vegetable oil

2 large onions, sliced

1cm/½in root ginger, grated

8 garlic cloves, crushed

2 large tomatoes, finely chopped

3-4 bay leaves

1kg/2¼lb chicken, chopped into 12 pieces

½ tsp turmeric

Salt to taste

500ml/16fl oz water

100g/3½oz coriander leaves, finely chopped

Method

- Mix the red chillies, coriander seeds, cardamom, cloves, cinnamon, fennel seeds and peppercorns together.
- Dry roast the mixture and grind to a powder. Set aside.
- Heat the oil in a saucepan. Add the onions. Fry them on a medium heat till they turn brown.
- Add the ginger and garlic. Fry for a minute.
- Add the tomatoes, bay leaves and the ground red chillies-coriander seeds powder. Continue to fry for 2-3 minutes.
- Add the chicken, turmeric, salt and water. Mix well. Cover with a lid and simmer for 40 minutes, stirring at regular intervals.
- Garnish the chicken with the coriander leaves. Serve hot.

Kashmiri Chicken

Serves 4

Ingredients

2 tbsp malt vinegar

2 tsp chilli flakes

2 tsp mustard seeds

2 tsp cumin seeds

½ tsp black peppercorns

7.5cm/3in cinnamon

10 cloves

75g/2½oz ghee

1kg/2¼lb chicken, chopped into 12 pieces

1 tbsp refined vegetable oil

4 bay leaves

4 medium-sized onions, finely chopped

1 tbsp ginger paste

1 tbsp garlic paste

3 tomatoes, finely chopped

1 tsp turmeric

500ml/16fl oz water

Salt to taste

20 cashew nuts, ground

6 strands saffron soaked in the juice of 1 lemon

Method

- Mix the malt vinegar with the chilli flakes, mustard seeds, cumin seeds, peppercorns, cinnamon and cloves. Grind this mixture to a smooth paste. Set aside.
- Heat the ghee in a saucepan. Add the chicken pieces and fry them on a medium heat till they turn golden brown. Drain and set aside.
- Heat the oil in a saucepan. Add the bay leaves and onions. Fry this mixture on a medium heat till the onions turn brown.
- Add the vinegar paste. Mix well and cook this on a low heat for 7-8 minutes.
- Add the ginger paste and garlic paste. Fry this mixture for a minute.
- Add the tomatoes and turmeric. Mix thoroughly and cook on a medium heat for 2-3 minutes.
- Add the fried chicken, water and salt. Mix well to coat the chicken. Cover with a lid and simmer for 30 minutes, stirring occasionally.
- Add the cashew nuts and saffron. Continue to simmer for 5 minutes. Serve hot.

Rum 'n' Chicken

Serves 4

Ingredients

1 tsp garam masala

1 tsp chilli powder

1kg/2¼lb chicken, chopped into 8 pieces

6 garlic cloves

4 black peppercorns

4 cloves

½ tsp cumin seeds

2.5cm/1in cinnamon

50g/1¾oz fresh coconut, grated

4 almonds

1 green cardamom pod

1 tbsp coriander seeds

300ml/10fl oz water

75g/2½oz ghee

3 large onions, finely chopped

Salt to taste

½ tsp saffron

120ml/4fl oz dark rum

1 tbsp coriander leaves, finely chopped

Method

- Mix together the garam masala and the chilli powder. Marinate the chicken with this mixture for 2 hours.
- Dry roast the garlic, peppercorns, cloves, cumin seeds, cinnamon, coconut, almonds, cardamom and coriander seeds.
- Grind with 60ml/2fl oz water to a smooth paste. Set aside.
- Heat the ghee in a saucepan. Add the onions and fry them on a medium heat till they turn translucent.
- Add the garlic-peppercorn paste. Mix well. Fry the mixture for 3-4 minutes.
- Add the marinated chicken and the salt. Mix well. Continue to fry for 3-4 minutes, stirring occasionally.
- Add 240ml/8fl oz water. Stir gently. Cover with a lid and cook on a low heat for 40 minutes, stirring at regular intervals.
- Add the saffron and rum. Mix well and continue to simmer for 10 minutes.
- Garnish with the coriander leaves. Serve hot.

Chicken Shahjahani

(Chicken in Spicy Gravy)

Serves 4

Ingredients

5 tbsp refined vegetable oil

2 bay leaves

5cm/2in cinnamon

6 green cardamom pods

½ tsp cumin seeds

8 cloves

3 large onions, finely chopped

1 tsp turmeric

1 tsp chilli powder

1 tsp ginger paste

1 tsp garlic paste

Salt to taste

75g/2½oz cashew nuts, ground

150g/5½oz yoghurt, whisked

1kg/2¼lb chicken, chopped into 8 pieces

2 tbsp single cream

¼ tsp ground black cardamom

10g/¼oz coriander leaves, finely chopped

Method

- Heat the oil in a saucepan. Add the bay leaves, cinnamon, cardamom, cumin seeds and cloves. Let them splutter for 15 seconds.
- Add the onions, turmeric and chilli powder. Sauté the mixture on a medium heat for 1-2 minutes.
- Add the ginger paste and garlic paste. Fry for 2-3 minutes, stirring constantly.
- Add the salt and ground cashew nuts. Mix well and fry for another minute.
- Add the yoghurt and the chicken. Stir gently till the mixture coats the chicken pieces.
- Cover with a lid and cook the mixture on a low heat for 40 minutes, stirring at frequent intervals.
- Uncover the pan and add the cream and ground cardamom. Stir gently for 5 minutes.
- Garnish the chicken with the coriander leaves. Serve hot.

Easter Chicken

Serves 4

Ingredients

1 tsp lemon juice

1 tsp ginger paste

1 tsp garlic paste

Salt to taste

1kg/2¼lb chicken, chopped into 8 pieces

2 tbsp coriander seeds

12 garlic cloves

2.5cm/1in root ginger

1 tsp cumin seeds

8 red chillies

4 cloves

2.5cm/1in cinnamon

1 tsp turmeric

1 litre/1¾ pints water

4 tbsp refined vegetable oil

3 large onions, finely chopped

4 green chillies, slit lengthways

3 tomatoes, finely chopped

1 tsp tamarind paste

2 large potatoes, quartered

Method

- Mix the lemon juice, ginger paste, garlic paste and salt together. Marinate the chicken pieces with this mixture for 2 hours.
- Mix the coriander seeds, garlic, ginger, cumin seeds, red chillies, cloves, cinnamon and turmeric together.
- Grind this mixture with half the water to a smooth paste. Set aside.
- Heat the oil in a saucepan. Add the onions. Fry them on a medium heat till they turn translucent.
- Add the green chillies and the coriander seeds-garlic paste. Fry this mixture for 3-4 minutes.
- Add the tomatoes and the tamarind paste. Continue to fry for 2-3 minutes.
- Add the marinated chicken, potatoes and the remaining water. Mix thoroughly. Cover with a lid and simmer for 40 minutes, stirring at regular intervals.
- Serve hot.

Spicy Duck with Potatoes

Serves 4

Ingredients

1 tsp ground coriander

2 tsp chilli powder

¼ tsp turmeric

5cm/2in cinnamon

6 cloves

4 green cardamom pods

1 tsp fennel seeds

60ml/2fl oz refined vegetable oil

4 large onions, thinly sliced

5cm/2in root ginger, shredded

8 garlic cloves

6 green chillies, slit lengthways

3 large potatoes, quartered

1kg/2¼lb duck, chopped into 8-10 pieces

2 tsp malt vinegar

750ml/1¼ pints coconut milk

Salt to taste

1 tsp ghee

1 tsp mustard seeds

2 shallots, sliced

8 curry leaves

Method

- Mix the coriander, chilli powder, turmeric, cinnamon, cloves, cardamom and fennel seeds together. Grind this mixture to a powder. Set aside.
- Heat the oil in a saucepan. Add the onions, ginger, garlic and green chillies. Fry on a medium heat for 2-3 minutes.
- Add the spice mixture powder. Sauté for 2 minutes.
- Add the potatoes. Continue to fry for 3-4 minutes.
- Add the duck, malt vinegar, coconut milk and salt. Stir for 5 minutes. Cover with a lid and cook the mixture on a low heat for 40 minutes, stirring at frequent intervals. Once the duck is cooked, remove from the heat and set aside.
- Heat the ghee in a small saucepan. Add the mustard seeds, shallots and curry leaves. Stir-fry on a high heat for 30 seconds.
- Pour this over the duck. Mix well. Serve hot.

Duck Moile

(Simple Duck Curry)

Serves 4

Ingredients

1kg/2¼lb duck, chopped into 12 pieces

Salt to taste

1 tbsp ground coriander

1 tsp ground cumin

6 black peppercorns

4 cloves

2 green cardamom pods

2.5cm/1in cinnamon

120ml/4fl oz refined vegetable oil

3 large onions, finely chopped

5cm/2in root ginger, finely sliced

3 green chillies, finely chopped

½ tsp sugar

2 tbsp malt vinegar

360ml/12fl oz water

Method

- Marinate the duck pieces with the salt for an hour.
- Mix the ground coriander, ground cumin, peppercorns, cloves, cardamom and cinnamon together. Dry roast this mixture in a frying pan on a medium heat for 1-2 minutes.
- Remove from the heat and grind to a fine powder. Set aside.
- Heat the oil in a saucepan. Add the marinated duck pieces. Fry them on a medium heat till they turn brown. Turn occasionally to make sure that they do not burn. Drain and set aside.
- Heat the same oil and add the onions. Fry them on a medium heat till they turn brown.
- Add the ginger and green chillies. Continue to fry for 1-2 minutes.
- Add the sugar, malt vinegar and the coriander-cumin powder. Stir for 2-3 minutes.
- Add the fried duck pieces along with the water. Mix well. Cover with a lid and simmer for 40 minutes, stirring occasionally.
- Serve hot.

Bharwa Murgh Kaju

(Chicken Stuffed with Cashew Nuts)

Serves 4

Ingredients

3 tsp ginger paste

3 tsp garlic paste

10 cashew nuts, ground

1 tsp chilli powder

1 tsp garam masala

Salt to taste

8 chicken breasts, flattened

4 large onions, finely chopped

200g/7oz khoya*

6 green chillies, finely chopped

25g/scant 1oz mint leaves, finely chopped

25g/scant 1oz coriander leaves, finely chopped

2 tbsp lemon juice

75g/2½oz ghee

75g/2½oz cashew nuts, ground

400g/14oz yoghurt, whisked

2 tsp garam masala

2 tsp saffron, soaked in 2 tbsp warm milk

Salt to taste

Method

- Mix together half the ginger paste and half the garlic paste with the ground cashew nuts, chilli powder, garam masala and some salt.
- Marinate the chicken breasts with this mixture for 30 minutes.
- Mix half the onions with the khoya, green chillies, mint leaves, coriander leaves and lemon juice. Divide this mixture into 8 equal portions.
- Spread out a marinated chicken breast. Place a portion of the onion-khoya mixture on it. Roll like a wrap.

- Repeat this for the rest of the chicken breasts.
- Grease a baking dish and place the stuffed chicken breasts inside, with the loose ends face-down.
- Roast the chicken in an oven at 200°C (400°F, Gas Mark 6) for 20 minutes. Set aside.
- Heat the ghee in a saucepan. Add the remaining onions. Fry them on a medium heat till they turn translucent.

- Add the remaining ginger paste and garlic paste. Fry the mixture for 1-2 minutes.
- Add the ground cashew nuts, yoghurt and garam masala. Stir for 1-2 minutes.
- Add the roasted chicken rolls, saffron mixture and some salt. Mix well. Cover with a lid and cook on a low heat for 15-20 minutes. Serve hot.

Yoghurt Chicken Masala

Serves 4

Ingredients

1kg/2¼lb chicken, chopped into 12 pieces

7.5cm/3in root ginger, grated

10 garlic cloves, crushed

½ tsp chilli powder

½ tsp garam masala

½ tsp turmeric

2 green chillies

Salt to taste

200g/7oz yoghurt

½ tsp cumin seeds

1 tsp coriander seeds

4 cloves

4 black peppercorns

2.5cm/1in cinnamon

4 green cardamom pods

6-8 almonds

5 tbsp ghee

4 medium-sized onions, finely chopped

250ml/8fl oz water

1 tbsp coriander leaves, finely chopped

Method

- Pierce the chicken pieces with a fork. Set aside.
- Mix half the ginger and garlic with the chilli powder, garam masala, turmeric, green chillies and salt. Grind this mixture to a smooth paste. Whisk the paste with the yoghurt.
- Marinate the chicken with this mixture for 4-5 hours. Set aside.
- Heat a saucepan. Dry roast the cumin seeds, coriander seeds, cloves, peppercorns, cinnamon, cardamom and almonds. Set aside.

- Heat 4 tbsp of the ghee in a heavy saucepan. Add the onions. Fry them on a medium heat till they turn translucent.
- Add the remaining ginger and garlic. Fry for 1-2 minutes.
- Remove from the heat and grind this mixture with the dry roasted cumin-coriander mixture to a smooth paste.

- Heat the remaining ghee in a saucepan. Add the paste and fry it on a medium heat for 2-3 minutes.
- Add the marinated chicken and fry for another 3-4 minutes.
- Add the water. Stir gently for a minute. Cover with a lid and simmer for 30 minutes, stirring at regular intervals.
- Garnish with the coriander leaves and serve hot.